Understanding Data Science

Science

From Theory to Application

Table of Contents

Chapter 1. Introduction

Welcome to this Special Report titled, "Understanding Data Science: From Theory to Application." In this comprehensive study, we unravel the intricacies of data science and shed light on its theoretical framework and practical applications like never before. This report will take you on an enlightening journey through the world of data, where numbers shape narratives and trends dictate actions. We've distilled complex statistical theories into easy-to-understand concepts, making the daunting world of data science accessible to all. Whether you're an industry professional looking to upscale your analytic abilities, an academic seeking to broaden your research horizon, or simply a curious mind intrigued by data, this report offers a wealth of learning. Place yourself at the forefront of the data revolution, equipped with the knowledge to navigate the data-driven future. Are you ready to unlock the power of data?

Chapter 2. Unveiling Data Science: An Introduction

Data Science is an interdisciplinary field that utilizes scientific methods, processes, algorithms, and systems to extract knowledge and insights from structured and unstructured data. Predicated on statistics, mathematics, and computer science, data science gives a comprehensive view of data from various angles, converted into useful and consumable information.

2.1. What is Data Science?

Data science is a blend of various algorithms, tools, and machine learning principles that operate with the goal of discovering hidden patterns from raw data. It is a technique that extracts insights from data for both structured and unstructured forms and treats them to provide a fruitful result.

Data science is not about developing complex models or writing code. Instead, its potency lies in exploring information from multiple sources in various formats, then using business knowledge to drive valuable insights. With data science, you can reach anywhere across the business horizon, making the field compelling and innovative.

2.2. The Intersection of Different Fields

Data science is at the intersection of numerous fields. Three predominant regions build up the structure of data science:

1. Mathematics and Statistics: The backbone of any data operation, the algorithms developed and used for extracting information are derived from mathematical principles and statistical theorems.

2. Domain Knowledge/ Business Intelligence: While the maths provides the tools, utilizing these tools effectively requires intensive industry knowledge.

3. Computer Science/Information Technology: Since these analyses are performed on a computer, effective coding skills in languages like Python, R, or SAS combined with an understanding of databases are essential.

2.3. Need for Data Science

The fourth Industrial Revolution has ramped up the generation of data, necessitating a system in place to manage and analyze it. With data coming from different sources in different formats, employing standard business intelligence tools became insufficient.

Data science came into the picture to engage with this massive influx of data — the promising oil of the 21st Century. From optimizing search engines to understanding consumer behavior, predicting weather forecasts to improving healthcare delivery, data science seeps into every bit of modern life.

2.4. The Process of Data Science

Data Science is a step-by-step process that represents, visualizes, and models data insights. Let's delve into these detailed steps:

1. Frame the problem: The first step is to identify and clearly articulate the problem to be solved, establishing objectives.

2. Collect the raw data: Once the problem is defined, the next step involves gathering raw data pertinent to the problem.

3. Process the data: This phase involves transforming raw data into an understandable format, removing abnormalities, inconsistencies and ensuring data is clean and usable.

4. Explore the data: In this exploratory analysis, you aim to understand the underlying patterns and trends in your data.

5. Model the data: Once you understand your data, build models using algorithms for prediction or classification purposes.

6. Communicate: Once models are set, results should be communicated effectively, often through data visualizations and reports.

2.5. Tools of Data Science

Data science uses an array of tools, including SQL databases, programming languages like Python and R, and data visualization tools such as Tableau or PowerBI. In addition, various machine learning platforms like TensorFlow or PyTorch facilitate even more advanced analyses.

2.6. The Impact of Data Science

Data Science is playing a crucial role in the advancement of technologies. Websites recommending you products or movies based on your past behavior, self-driving cars, voice assistants replicating human interactions, fraudulent banking transactions being immediately flagged - all rely heavily on data science.

While companies across sectors are reaping benefits through increased profitability, efficiency, and competitiveness, society at large is also gaining through improved healthcare systems, enhanced public policy, and better disaster management.

To summarize, data science is here to stay. It's a promising field that has transformed the way businesses operate and decisions made, pushing everyone to become data-driven. By exploring and understanding the profound implications of this field, we learn more than just a new technical skill-set. We gain a tool to shape our world.

As Tom Forester once pointedly wrote, "Computers are incredibly fast, accurate, and stupid. Human beings are incredibly slow, inaccurate, and brilliant. Together they are powerful beyond imagination." Let's embrace this synergistic relationship and journey ahead.

Chapter 3. Diving Deep into Data: Types & Sources

1. Understanding Data

To completely appreciate the capabilities of data science, we must first lay our foundation on the groundwork of data basics. Data, in the simplest terms, is a collection of facts or information. In today's digitally-driven era, data can be quantitative, qualitative, big or small, however, all data is not created equal. Data can be classified into several categories based on various attributes including structure, source, and type of content.

Quantitative data and qualitative data represent the two main types of data used in statistics and research, with a third type — mixed methods data, which is a combination of the two.

3.1. Quantitative Data

Quantitative data is numerical and can be counted, measured, or expressed using numbers. Quantitative data is often called structured data and is typically collected in a systematic manner from experiments, surveys, and so on. It is data in a format that can be analyzed using mathematical and statistical techniques. Some common examples are census data, such as age or income—the data is numerical and can be sorted into categories or ranked in order. Other examples include temperatures or weights—again these numbers can be ordered and differences calculated.

Quantitative data can be further classified into continuous and discrete data. Continuous data represents measurements and therefore can take on any value in a given range. Examples include height, weight, temperature, the amount of sugar in an orange, or the time required to run a mile. Discrete data, on the other hand, represents counts and can only take on particular values. Examples include the number of students in a class, the number of lions in a wildlife reserve, or the number of patients in a hospital.

3.2. Qualitative Data

Qualitative data, otherwise known as categorical or nominal data, is non-numerical and is used to describe information that does not have a numeric value. It is often used in exploratory research to understand underlying reasons, opinions, and motivations, providing insights into the problem that help develop ideas or hypotheses for potential quantitative research. Qualitative data can be collected through methods such as individual depth interviews, focus groups, ethnographic research, content/document analysis, and through the collection of case studies and reports from all levels of management.

Qualitative data can be further classified into ordinal, nominal, and dichotomous. Ordinal data are categorical data in which the categories have a meaningful order or ranking. Nominal data are categorical data in which categories do not have a meaningful order or ranking. Dichotomous or binary data is a special type of nominal data with only two categories.

3.3. Mixed Methods Data

Mixed methods data is a methodology characterized by the collection, analysis, and integration of both quantitative and qualitative data within a single study. It combines the collection or analysis of both closed-ended (quantitative) and open-ended (qualitative) data. This approach to research assumes that the combination of both types of data provides a more complete understanding of a research problem than either approach alone.

II. Sources of Data

The quality of any data-driven endeavor is heavily dependent on the quality of the data itself. The source from where data is found or collected can have a significant impact on the outcome of data analysis. Data sources can be broadly categorized into primary and secondary sources.

3.4. Primary Data Sources

Primary data is data collected first hand, directly by the researcher(s) for the specific purpose or research question at hand. Examples of methods for collecting primary data include observations, surveys, interviews, and experiments.

3.5. Secondary Data Sources

Secondary data, on the other hand, is data that has already been collected by someone else for a purpose other than the current research project. Secondary data sources include data that is already published and is publicly available or data that is internal to the organization such as sales data, financial data, operations-related data, etc. Some of the most common sources of secondary data include government publications, websites, books, journal articles, internal records of the organization, etc.

In the digital age, this distinction blurs as data often transcends the boundaries of primary and secondary classification. Traditional data sources are rapidly being supplemented or replaced by newer, wide-ranging data from websites, smart devices, social media, cloud computing environments, and other digital platforms.

The explosive growth in data usage and the vast range of data sources create dynamic opportunities for extraction of insights, but they also present challenges related to the robust management, security, privacy, and governance of data. In the subsequent chapters of this report, we will delve into these topics in much more detail. For now, suffice it to say that understanding the types and sources of data is our first step into the captivating world of data science.

Chapter 4. Foundational Theory of Data Science

The marvel of Data Science lies in an intricate web of theories, principles and techniques, drawn from various fields such as mathematics, statistics, information science, and computer science. To fully appreciate and utilize the potential of Data Science, one must first understand the theoretical underpinnings that lay the groundwork for all its applications.

4.1. Mathematics and Statistics

The foundation of Data Science starts with Mathematics and Statistics. Statistics, in its classical form, helps with the interpretation of data. It provides measures of central tendency (like mean, mode, and median), measures of dispersion (like range, variance, and standard deviation), and probability distributions (like Normal, Binomial, and Poisson), all of which are fundamental to understanding data.

Mathematics, particularly linear algebra and calculus, also play an essential role in understanding data at scale. Linear algebra allows for the manipulation of data structures, and calculus helps optimize machine learning models. For example, concepts such as matrix algebra and eigenvalues/vectors form the theoretical basis for Principal Component Analysis (PCA), one of the most popular techniques for dimensionality reduction in high-dimensional datasets.

4.2. Information Theory

Another significant theoretical basis of Data Science is Information Theory, a branch of applied mathematics concerning data compression and error detection. Entropy, a central concept from this field, quantifies the amount of uncertainty or randomness in a set of data.

In Data Science, entropy is typically used for features selection, which pertains to selecting relevant features from a dataset to create a model. It is instrumental in decision tree algorithms, where features with low entropy are preferred as they lead to more definite conclusions.

4.3. Computer Science

Computer Science provides the tools and techniques required to store, process, and analyze large volumes of data. Big Data technologies like Hadoop and Spark are built on foundations of distributed computing principles, while algorithms and data structures provide efficient ways to process and analyze data.

Programming languages like Python and R have been optimized to work with data, providing libraries and frameworks that make it easy to implement statistical methods and machine learning algorithms. Understanding the operations of these languages and their underpinning computational logic is crucial in leveraging them to build robust data models.

4.4. Probability and Bayesian Theory

Probability theory, especially Bayesian probability, is instrumental in Data Science. It offers a systematic method to update our beliefs about an event occurring based on evidence. This is instrumental in many machine learning models, especially in Naive Bayes and Bayesian Networks.

4.5. Machine Learning Theory

Last but not least, Machine Learning Theory forms a critical part of the theoretical foundation of Data Science. Machine learning is a type of artificial intelligence that allows software applications to become more accurate in predicting outcomes without being explicitly programmed to do so.

4.6. Understanding Bias-Variance Tradeoff

A critical theoretical concept in model building is the Bias-Variance Tradeoff. Too simple a model and it underfits the data (high bias), too complex, and it overfits (high variance). The tradeoff is an essential principle in model selection and evaluation. Another notable theory here is the 'No Free Lunch' theorem, which posits that no single model works best for every problem.

To navigate the landscape of Data Science with expertise, it is imperative to delve deep into these areas of theory, comprehend their intricacies, and understand their real-world applications. If we can unlock this understanding, data no longer remains just a mere collection of numbers; it becomes a potent tool for insight, prediction, and often, revolution.

While this chapter focuses on theoretical aspects, it's crucial to extend this knowledge to practical application in the field. The world of data science is ever-evolving, and applied theory is the bridge that will enable you to stay on top of these ongoing changes.

Bringing all these theories together and comprehending them holistically, one not only gains expertise in handling data but also acquires the ability to harness the full potential of data science. Remember, theoretical understanding and practical application go hand in hand to form a complete data scientist.

Chapter 5. Statistical Inference: Learning from Data

To truly unlock the power of data, one must understand and adeptly use statistical inference – the process of extracting valuable insights from data. It's through this rigorous process that all data-driven decisions are made. This chapter delves into the theoretical fundamentals and practical applications of this foundational aspect of data science.

5.1. The Essence of Statistical Inference

The fundamental idea behind statistical inference is drawing conclusions, generalizations, or decisions about a population based on a sample of data from said population. The process might involve forming a predictive model, estimating parameters, or testing a hypothesis. Interested in knowing the average height of men in a country? Measure a representative sample. Want to ascertain whether a certain type of medicine is effective? Sample tests are conducted, and based on the observed results, an assertion is made.

There are two main types of statistical inference: estimation and hypothesis testing.

5.2. Estimation

Estimation is a statistical inference method used to determine the likely value of a population parameter (such as mean, median, or mode) based on a random sample from that population. There are two types of estimation processes: point estimation and interval estimation.

Point estimation attempts to provide the single best prediction of some quantity of interest. For example, we might want to estimate the population mean, μ. The sample mean, $x\Box$, is a good point estimate of μ.

Interval estimation provides a range of possible values for the parameter, which incorporates a probability statement about the degree of confidence that the parameter lies within the interval. For instance, instead of estimating that the average score for an exam was 70, an interval estimator might suggest it is between 65 and 75 with 95% confidence.

5.3. Hypothesis Testing

Hypothesis testing is a systematic way to test claims or ideas about a group or population using sample data. A hypothesis test evaluates two mutually exclusive statements about a population to determine which statement is best supported by the sample data.

The two competing hypotheses are often called the null hypothesis (denoted by H0) and the alternative hypothesis (denoted by Ha or H1). The null hypothesis is the initial statistical claim that we assume to be correct. The alternative hypothesis is the opposite of the null hypothesis. It's what we are testing for.

A common approach to hypothesis testing is the P-value approach. A P-value is a probability that provides a measure of the strength of evidence against the null hypothesis provided by the sample. Lower p-values provide stronger evidence against the null hypothesis.

5.4. Key Concepts in Statistical Inference

It's essential to understand certain concepts prerequisite to utilizing statistical inference effectively. They include:

- Standard Error: The standard deviation of the sampling distribution.

- Central Limit Theorem: It states that the sampling distribution of the sample mean approximates a normal distribution, regardless of the shape of the population distribution, as the sample size grows larger.

- Confidence Interval: A range of values, derived from a data set, that is likely to contain the value of an estimate of interest.

- Level of Significance: The probability of rejecting the null hypothesis when it is true. Commonly denoted as α.

5.5. Practical Applications: Statistical Inference in Action

Statistical inference is applicable in various fields. In medicine, it enables us to identify the efficacy of treatments and understand the spread of diseases. Marketers use statistical inference to understand consumer behavior and make strategic decisions. In finance, statistical inferences help estimate future stock prices and manage risks. Social scientists use these methods to comprehend individual and group behaviors. These are but a few instances of the immense potential that statistical inference holds.

Overall, robust understanding and effective use of statistical inference are crucial for any data scientist, statistician, researcher, analyst, or any professional who wants to draw meaningful and useful insights from data – to turn noise into narratives, randomness into rhythm.

Chapter 6. Data Mining and Machine Learning: The Heart of Data Science

Understanding data science is an exercise in multidisciplinary learning. It combines areas of expertise such as statistics, information technology, and specific domain knowledge, among others. One of the primary areas of this confluence is the realm of Data Mining and Machine Learning. These are the engines that power the data science vehicle, driving it forward and enhancing its capacity.

6.1. Understanding Data Mining

Data mining is the investigative process of finding and illustrating unknown patterns and details within large sets of structured and unstructured data. Essentially, it is synonymous with 'knowledge discovery in databases,' and seeks to extract high-quality information from our vast volumes of data.

This insightful journey through databases begins with data preprocessing. This is key to preparing data by cleaning it (rectifying or removing erroneous data) and normalizing it (setting ranges for data attributes). Additionally, data is transformed to ensure consistency and converted into the appropriate format for efficient mining.

Once preprocessing is complete, the data mining phase begins. This involves different techniques such as:

1. Association rules (identifying sets of items occurring together)
2. Classification (predictive modelling to identify data classes)

3. Clustering (delineating groups with similar behaviour)

4. Anomaly Detection (identifying outliers)

Post-mining, results are evaluated and represented visually for better understanding. This iterative process continues as new data emerges and old data evolves, modifying patterns and revealing new ones.

6.2. Delving Deeper: The Methods of Data Mining

Data mining techniques are a blend of statistical methods, mathematical algorithms, and machine learning. Let's delve further into some widely used methods.

Sequential pattern mining, for instance, involves identifying similar patterns or trends in transaction data over a certain period. This is extensively used in market basket analysis, where combinations of products frequently bought together are identified.

Another interesting technique is regression analysis, a statistical method used to determine the strength and character of the relationship between one dependent variable and a series of other variables. Logistic regressions, for instance, are used in machine learning and the field of data mining to predict the probability of categorical dependent variables.

6.3. Introduction to Machine Learning

Machine learning is a subset of artificial intelligence. It empowers computer systems to learn from data, identify patterns, and make decisions with minimal human intervention. Machine learning is the quintessential fuel that powers data mining processes.

There are broadly three types of machine learning: supervised, unsupervised, and reinforcement learning.

6.4. Supervised Learning

In supervised learning, the model learns from a labeled dataset. Each data point in the training dataset has an assigned output. The goal of the model is to find the mapping function from the input variables to the output. Examples of supervised learning include linear regression and support vector machines (SVM).

6.5. Unsupervised Learning

Unsupervised learning, in contrast, does not have any labeled data points. The model learns to identify patterns and structures in the input data. One common application of this is in clustering, where the model groups similar data. K-means clustering is a popular method in this category.

6.6. Reinforcement Learning

In reinforcement learning, an agent learns how to behave in an environment by performing actions and observing their results. The agent is 'rewarded' or 'punished' depending on the action's outcome. Reinforcement learning has been successfully used in game play and robotics.

6.7. Machine Learning Algorithms and their Applications

A critical component to understanding machine learning is becoming familiar with its popular algorithms and their areas of application.

Decision trees, for example, are exceptionally effective at solving classification and regression tasks. They are simple, yet powerful, and visualize decision rules gleaned from data. Decision trees' visual appeal and simplicity have made them popular in fields as diverse as healthcare, finance, and marketing.

Random forest, an ensemble of decision trees, reduces the risk of overfitting and is robust to noise. It holds a firm position in recommendation engines used by Netflix and Amazon.

Another popular technique is logistic regression, which uses a logistic function to model a binary dependent variable. In the medical field, it is used to predict diseases based on observations. In marketing, it has applications like predicting the likelihood of a customer's purchase.

6.8. The Confluence of Data Mining and Machine Learning

Data mining and machine learning flow seamlessly into each other. They both thrive on the principle of 'learning from data'. While data mining seeks to uncover hidden patterns and associations in vast data stores, machine learning leverages these discoveries to learn and adapt over time. This confluence forms the heart of data science.

Summing it up, data mining provides a starting platform, the exploratory tool in the world of data. Machine learning takes this a step further, utilizing the explored data and extracting actionable insights. Together, they enable intelligent decision-making and predictive capabilities, contributing to organizations' strategic and operational excellence. The power of data is truly unlocked when these two join hands.

6.9. The Future: Big Data, Deep Learning, and Beyond

Looking at the evolutionary journey of data mining and machine learning, it's clear that we're on the brink of transformative breakthroughs.

Big Data's advent heralds an era where the amount and variety of data is unprecedented. This data deluge necessitates enhanced mining techniques and robust machine learning algorithms capable of handling such voluminous data.

Additionally, the emergence of deep learning - a subset of machine learning, has made it possible for computers to understand and interpret complex patterns and structures in data. Deep learning is especially effective in dealing with image and speech recognition and is poised to make significant contributions to artificial intelligence in the coming years.

Whether it's unraveling truths hidden deep within databases or making enigmatic machine learning concepts clearer, the trail to understanding data science is as enlightening as it is exciting. With data mining and machine learning as its heart, data science is a journey of turning raw data quantities into a quality understanding, a complex voyage of discovery within the numeric world around us. This is where trends dictate action, narratives are shaped by numbers, and tomorrow is prepared today.

Indeed, with the knowledge you acquire, stand ready to shape the world- the data-driven future beckons.

Stay curious. Stay informed. Keep mining. Keep learning.

Chapter 7. Data Wrangling and Visualization: Making Sense of Raw Data

Data wrangling, often referred to as data munging, is the process of converting or mapping data from its raw form into another format that allows for more convenient consumption of the data. This step is arguably a fundamental part of the data science pipeline because it prepares the 'once crude' information for ensuing exploration and analysis. As such, the emphasis on quality data wrangling cannot be overstated. A project's overall success often depends on the careful upfront work done to cleanse and organize the data; in fact, reports suggest that data scientists spend approximately 60% of their time on this/data wrangling.

Visualization, on the other hand, is the presentation of data in a pictorial or graphical format. It ensures the complicated data sets are communicated effectively and understood by people with varying expertise levels. It's a critical exploratory tool and an essential component for impacting the decision-making process.

7.1. The Process of Data Wrangling

Data wrangling is generally made up of several stages; these include data acquisition, data cleaning, and data transformation. Understanding these steps provides insight into the whole data wrangling process and the essential role it plays in gaining meaningful insights.

Data Acquisition: This is the process of gathering and importing data for immediate use or future use. The data can come in various formats such as text files, Excel files, SQL databases, web APIs, and scraping website data. The type of data determines the acquisition method.

Data Cleaning: Undoubtedly, the data you acquire will have inconsistencies, errors, or missing parts. These could be due to various reasons, including data entry errors, missing values, and incorrect formatting. The data cleaning process includes handling these anomalies; it helps improve the quality and reliability of datasets.

Data Transformation: Once we have cleaned the data, the next step in the data wrangling process is to convert raw data into another format that's more appropriate for consumption. This might involve manipulating raw data using arithmetic operations, normalizing data, or grouping and aggregating data.

7.2. Using Python for Data Wrangling

Python is a popular language in data science due to its simplicity and wide range of libraries designed to manipulate and investigate data. Two essential libraries for data wrangling are Pandas and NumPy.

Pandas is a powerful Python library often used for data manipulation and analysis. It provides data structures and functions needed to manipulate structured data, including functions for reading and writing data between different file formats.

NumPy, short for Numerical Python, is used for numerical computations and working with arrays. It also integrates with Pandas, making it easy to clean, transform, and analyze data.

7.3. Data Visualization and Its Importance

Effective data visualization conveys a story that words or raw numbers cannot express. Incorporating visualization into the data analysis process allows your target audience to derive insights from the data in an easily understandable way.

Moreover, visualization presents patterns, trends, and correlations that might go unnoticed in traditional reports. It makes insights much more digestible, especially for a non-technical audience.

When working with Python, matplotlib is the most used library for creating static, animated, and interactive visualizations. Another popular choice is seaborn, which is essentially a high-level interface to matplotlib. It has a higher-level and more convenient API, making it easier to create complex visualizations.

7.4. Creating Infographics Using Python

Infographics are a highly effective data visualization tool. They allow the reader to understand complex information quickly and clearly. Python has different libraries such as matplotlib, seaborn, and plotly that make creating infographics possible.

In sum, data wrangling and visualization are instrumental in turning raw data into understandable, useable information. They're integral parts of the data science pipeline, bridging the gap between raw data and insightful decision making. The ability to efficiently wrangle and visualize data is indispensable in modern organizations, helping to turn the complex into simple, the confusing into clear, and the unknown into known.

Chapter 8. Predictive Analytics: Forecasting the Future

In the world of data science, predictive analysis holds a unique position as it offers a glimpse into the future. By employing a wide range of statistical techniques and algorithms, predictive analytics enables businesses and organizations to understand potential future events by analyzing past data.

Think of predictive analytics as a crystal ball in the hands of data scientists and analysts. But, this crystal ball doesn't run on magic - instead, it leverages a wide array of algorithms, statistical analysis, machine learning techniques, and data mining to extract the insightful patterns hidden underneath heaps of data and generate reliable potential outcomes.

8.1. Understanding Predictive Analytics

Predictive analytics revolves around the idea of leveraging the past to foretell the future. How, though? It's pretty straightforward. Every event in the world, when happens, leaves behind an extensive dataset. This dataset, when analyzed with the right techniques, unveils patterns. These patterns and trends are then applied to future scenarios, resulting in a reliable prediction.

8.2. Components of Predictive Analytics

Predictive analytics consists of three key components -

1. Data: This includes historical and transactional data, as well as real-time feed.

2. Statistical Analysis Techniques: This includes a variety of statistical analysis techniques like regression analysis, multivariate statistics, decision tree, and others.

3. Assumptions: This involves considering certain events or conditions that may influence the future event one is trying to predict.

8.3. The Predictive Analytic Process

The predictive analysis process starts with defining the project outcomes, business objectives, and delving into each phase in detail.

Step 1: Project Definition

The first step is to understand the business objectives, identify the key stakeholders, define the scope of the project, and outline the deliverables.

Step 2: Data Collection

The success of predictive analysis hinges on the quality and quantity of data gathered. This data can come from a multitude of sources, including transactions, log files, sensors, external feeds, and other structured and unstructured sources.

Step 3: Data Analysis

This step entails the rigorous cleaning, transforming, and analyzing of the data collected. This reveals meaningful insights and trends within the data.

Step 4: Statistical Analysis

This phase involves implementing standard statistical techniques in order to further study and visualize data. The model for prediction is then created using these techniques.

Step 5: Model Verification

In this step, the model is verified and validated for its effectiveness. The model's assumptions and outcomes are scrutinized and measured against predetermined criteria.

Step 6: Deployment

Once verified, the model is then deployed into the decision-making process.

Step 7: Model Monitoring

Once deployed, the model needs regular monitoring and fine-tuning in order to ensure its relevance and validity over time.

8.4. Importance of Predictive Analytics

In today's competitive business landscape, predictive analytics has become a game changer. Whether it's understanding customer behavior to deliver personalized experiences, managing resources, detecting frauds or predicting market trends, predictive analytics strengthens decision making.

Predictive analytics allows organizations to anticipate outcomes and behaviors based on data and not merely on assumptions. This leads to more strategic and knowledgeable decision making, which in turn can drive greater operational efficiency, reduce risks, and enhance marketing tactics.

The true power of predictive analytics lies in its ability to identify insights and trends that are not immediately apparent. Moreover, it helps in uncovering patterns in areas such as customer behavior, product performance, operational abilities, market trends and demographics - just to name a few.

8.5. Challenges in Predictive Analytics

While predictive analytics promises a wealth of benefits, it also comes with its own set of challenges. These are predominantly around data privacy, data quality, and the skills required to handle complex algorithms and models.

1. Data privacy: With the rising awareness around data privacy and the enforcement of regulations like GDPR, it's essential to ensure the data's confidentiality while using predictive analytics.

2. Data quality: Quality of data is a critical concern. Accurate prediction models demand high-quality, relevant data. Faulty data can result in misleading predictions.

3. Skillset: The ability to understand and operate advanced algorithms and machine learning models requires a specialized skill set and sophisticated software.

Despite these challenges, predictive analytics, combining the power of data and technology, continues to secure its position as a critical tool in any data scientist's arsenal, illuminating the pathway to strategic decision making and operational efficiency. As we continue to generate vast amounts of data, the potential of predictive analytics in realizing a data-driven future remains immense.

In conclusion, through predictive analytics, data science not only tells a story about the past, but it also provides a probable script for the future. It is important to understand that predictive analytics does not guarantee the future but nudges us closer towards predicting it with accuracy, giving us unique advantages and fresh perspectives.

Chapter 9. Big Data and Cloud Computing: Managing Voluminous Data

The concept of 'Big Data' has gained immense popularity over the past few decades, and for good reason. Big data refers to an enormous volume of structured and unstructured data that inundates businesses daily. The sheer volume of this data challenges the traditional methods of data processing. It not only revolves around the size of the data, but also focuses on the velocity, variety, veracity, and value—the 5Vs that describe its properties.

In this context, Cloud computing has emerged as a game-changing solution. Cloud computing is an on-demand model for network access, where resources like networks, servers, storage, applications, and services are provided as metered services over the internet.

9.1. The 5Vs of Big Data

Before delving into the interaction between Big Data and Cloud Computing, it's important to understand the 5Vs of Big Data: Volume, Velocity, Variety, Veracity, and Value.

- **Volume**: This refers to the massive amount of data generated every second from various sources like social media, business transactions, science experiments, and more.
- **Velocity**: This represents the speed at which data is created, stored, processed, and analyzed.
- **Variety**: This describes the different types of data (structured, semi-structured, and unstructured) that are generated from various sources.
- **Veracity**: This refers to the quality and reliability of data. Due to

the large amount of data, it's challenging to ensure that all data is accurate and trustworthy.

- **Value**: This is the ability to turn data into valuable information that can aid decision-making.

9.2. Big Data Management: The Challenges

Big data management presents numerous challenges, predominantly due to the 5Vs. Storing large volumes of data, processing it swiftly (velocity), handling a vast array of data types (variety), ensuring data quality (veracity), and extracting meaningful insights (value), all pose formidable tasks.

Traditional data processing tools lack the power and speed to handle vast amounts of data and extract relevant information. Also, data security and privacy is paramount, adding another level of complexity.

9.3. Cloud Computing to the Rescue

This is where Cloud Computing plays a crucial role. It provides scalable and on-demand computing resources which are essential for storing and processing big data. Cloud platforms offer large-scale computing power, virtually limitless storage, and advanced analytics tools that can process vast datasets in real-time.

Cloud computing can be categorized into three main service models:

- **Infrastructure as a Service (IaaS)**: This provides the infrastructure such as virtual machines and other resources like virtual-machine disk image library, block and file-based storage, firewalls, load balancers, IP addresses, virtual local area networks etc.

- **Platform as a Service (PaaS)**: This is used for applications, and other development, while providing cloud components to software. This includes development tools, database management, business intelligence (BI) services, etc.

- **Software as a Service (SaaS)**: In this service model, the cloud-based applications are provided to the user, as a service on demand. It is a single instance of the service running on the cloud and multiple end users are serviced.

These models, along with specific services like Data as a Service (DaaS), provide flexible, scalable, and cost-effective solutions for big data management.

9.4. Benefits of Cloud Computing for Big Data

Combining Cloud computing with Big data not only solves the problem of data volume but also offers an array of advantages.

- **Scalability**: Cloud platforms offer virtually unlimited and scalable storage and processing power to handle the ever-increasing volume of data.

- **Cost-effectiveness**: With Cloud computing, organizations can save significant capital expenditure on infrastructure setup and maintenance.

- **Speed and Agility**: Cloud-based analytics can deliver results in real-time, enabling businesses to gain insights faster and make timely decisions.

- **Flexibility**: With Cloud, organizations can choose to scale up or down, based on their needs. They can also choose from different service models and deployment models as per their requirement.

9.5. Mitigating Big Data Challenges with Cloud Computing

Addressing the challenges of Big Data using Cloud Computing techniques involves the integration of various strategies and technologies.

Data storage and processing necessitate powerful, distributed computing systems that can handle vast volumes at speed. To this end, technologies such as the Hadoop ecosystem and NoSQL databases have made significant impact. Hadoop, with its powerful MapReduce function and distributed file system (HDFS), has proven to be efficient in handling large datasets across clusters of computers.

In the realm of data security, strict protocols and advanced encryption techniques are employed to ensure that data remains secure in transfer and at rest. Role-based access control (RBAC), data anonymization, and intrusion detection systems are among the numerous security measures adopted.

On the issue of data variety, advanced analytics tools capable of processing structured and unstructured data helps organizations make sense out of the data chaos. Natural Language Processing (NLP) and machine learning algorithms are used to draw insights from unstructured text, images, audio, and video.

Finally, data veracity is ensured by rigorous data validation and cleaning measures. Data cleansing tools and data quality software play key roles in maintaining high data integrity.

To conclude, it can certainly be said that the amalgamation of Big Data with Cloud Computing is a potent combination. This fusion not only addresses the challenges of managing voluminous data but also empowers organizations to leverage data to its fullest potential. With continuous advancements in technology, the synergy of Big Data and Cloud Computing is anticipated to grow even stronger, heralding a new era of data-driven decision-making and business intelligence.

Chapter 10. Real-World Applications of Data Science

Data Science, as a multidisciplinary field, uses scientific methods, processes, algorithms, and systems to extract knowledge and insights from structured and unstructured data. In the real world, its applications are vast, varied, and consequential – impacting industries and operations across the spectrum. Here, we look at several key fields where data science plays a pivotal role.

10.1. Healthcare

In healthcare, data science has brought in a paradigm shift. Predictive analytics and machine learning algorithms help anticipate disease outbreaks, devise treatment plans, and optimize patient care. Additionally, genomics leverages these approaches to decode complex diseases, driving breakthroughs in precision medicine.

For instance, the analysis of Electronic Health Records (EHR) using machine learning allows healthcare professionals to predetermine health risks, refine diagnoses, and establish personalized treatments. This approach bridges the gap between a physician's intuition and data-supported decisions.

Simultaneously, medical imaging uses sophisticated image processing algorithms, including deep learning techniques, for detecting abnormalities, thereby assisting more accurate and timely diagnoses. For instance, the convolutional neural network (CNN), a deep learning algorithm, is innovatively employed to analyze visual imagery, such as scans of tumors.

10.2. Financial Services

The financial sector heavily relies on data science to strategize investment, manage assets, assess risks, and prevent fraud. Machine learning algorithms – coupled with predictive modelling – empower financial institutions like banks and insurance companies to forecast market trends and make data-driven decisions.

Still, real-time analytics is tremendously vital in intra-day trading where fledgeling changes could lead to substantial financial implications. The ability to instantaneously process and interpret a vast amount of financial data gives firms a competitive advantage.

Also, with numerous transactions happening each minute, fraud detection has become a quintessential requirement. Anomaly detection techniques help identify unusual patterns or outliers in the data, enabling quick detection of fraudulent activities.

10.3. E-commerce

E-commerce platforms harness the power of data science to offer personalized experiences, drive customer engagement, and boost sales. Recommender systems analyze past user behavior and preferences to generate personalized recommendations.

Alongside, sentiment analysis, an application of Natural Language Processing (NLP), helps understand customer opinions and feedback to enhance the shopping experience. By identifying patterns in customer reviews, brands strive to improve their products and services.

Customer segmentation—categorizing customers based on their behaviour, demographics, and purchase history—assist in target marketing and creating personalized customer interactions.

10.4. Transportation and Logistics

In transportation and logistics, data science optimizes routes, reduces operating costs, improves supply chain efficiency, and enhances safety measures. GPS data, traffic data, and real-time tracking enable sophisticated analytics for optimal route planning.

Predictive analytics is leveraged to anticipate potential maintenance issues, thereby reducing unexpected equipment downtime—an application known as predictive maintenance.

Supply chain optimization uses various techniques such as simulation, forecasting, and predictive modelling to synchronize supply with demand, ensuring minimal wastage and increased efficiency.

10.5. Public Policy and Governance

Data Science assists public policy and governance by enabling informed decision-making, increasing transparency, and promoting citizen engagement. AI-driven sentiment analysis of social media platforms and news outlets assist in policy formulation based on the citizens' sentiment towards issues.

On a larger scale, big data is used for urban planning—with location data and satellite imagery aiding smart city initiatives, ensuring sustainability, and improving public amenities.

In the realm of government operations, data analytics tools help detect tax fraud and enforce compliance, resulting in increased revenue for public services.

Data science, therefore, pervades every element of our world today. From healthcare to finance, transportation to e-commerce, governance to public policy, its applications are transforming industries and creating opportunities for increased efficiency, reliability, and precision. In harnessing the potential of data science, pioneers across sectors are changing not just industry paradigms but also improving lives.

Chapter 11. Future Trends in Data Science

As we evolve in this data-driven era, many future trends will shape the nature and implications of data science. Let's delve into what's forthcoming in the realm of data science.

11.1. The Rising Dominance of Big Data

Growth in data has been exponential. IBM indicates that 90% of the data available now has been generated in just the last two years. This influx of data, popularly referred to as Big Data, plays a dynamic role in influencing data science trends. With greater availability of data, there are new and better opportunities for machine learning, predictive analytics, personalized services, and much more.

11.2. Evolution of Artificial Intelligence

Artificial Intelligence (AI) has been a buzzword for years now, but its practical applications and capabilities keep evolving. AI and machine learning are transforming businesses through targeted customer service, anomaly detection, and other services. As computational power increases, we can expect AI to become more intelligent, self-learning, and responsive. AI will influence the way we process and interact with data, making it more accessible and insightful.

11.3. Quantum Computing in Data Science

Quantum computing, although in its nascent stages, holds immense promise for data science. It aims to solve complex problems by leveraging the principles of quantum mechanics, thereby vastly enhancing computational speed and efficiency. As quantum computing matures, it can potentially transform the way data is stored, processed, and utilized, thus revolutionizing various facets of data science.

11.4. Automation of Data Science Tasks

We are already witnessing the automation of certain data science tasks. This trend will further proliferate as automation technologies mature. From data cleaning and preprocessing to model selection and hyperparameter tuning, automation is poised to streamline data science and render it more efficient. Such advancement will lead to quicker insights and enable data scientists to focus on more intricate problems.

11.5. The Importance of Data Privacy and Security

While greater access to data has several advantages, it simultaneously exacerbates privacy and security concerns. The increasing incidence of data breaches has underscored the importance of data privacy and security. Hence, in the future, efficient data science practices will require robust data security measures. This aspect will expectantly give rise to secure data environments and better encryption techniques.

11.6. Augmented Analytics

Augmented analytics combines AI and machine learning techniques to automate insights generation into data. It employs natural language processing to deliver clear and actionable insights, facilitating business executives to make data-driven decisions more efficiently. As businesses strive for better insights with less effort, we are likely to see an increasing demand for augmented analytics.

11.7. Growing Need for Real-Time Data and Analytics

The digital landscape is moving towards real-time data analysis to facilitate instant decision making. Be it healthcare, finance, or e-commerce, real-time insights provide businesses a tangible advantage over competitors. This push for immediacy will influence the tools and strategies employed in data science.

11.8. The Emergence of Collaborative Data Science

The future of data science will also be marked by better collaboration between data experts. This means the development of platforms and environments that facilitate the sharing of insights and models, leading to a more effective approach to tackling complex problems. Data science will become less siloed and more of a team effort, leading to better outcomes and innovations.

11.9. Data Visualization

Alongside generating insights, the practice of representing data in a user-friendly and visual manner is also becoming imperative. As data visualization tools become more advanced, they are expected to play a crucial role in data science by making data interpretation and communication more effective and straightforward.

11.10. The Importance of Explainable AI

As AI-based models become more sophisticated, they also become more opaque, resulting in a black-box syndrome. Future trends in data science emphasize the importance of Explainable AI, which aims to make these models more transparent, explainable, and accountable.

In conclusion, the field of data science is set for even more dramatic changes in the coming years. As the amount and variety of data continue to grow, so will the opportunities and challenges tied to its use. From AI advancements and quantum computing to privacy concerns and data visualization, these are just a few trends shaping the metamorphosis of data science. It's an incredibly exciting time to be part of this vibrant field with a myriad of opportunities for both professionals and businesses alike. Regardless of what specific path data science takes in the coming years, one thing is clear – the future will be increasingly data-driven.

www.ingramcontent.com/pod-product-compliance
Lightning Source LLC
LaVergne TN
LVHW051627050326
832903LV00033B/4693